VIETNAM
the culture

Bobbie Kalman

A Bobbie Kalman Book

The Lands, Peoples, and Cultures Series

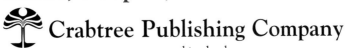

Crabtree Publishing Company

www.crabtreebooks.com

The Lands, Peoples, and Cultures Series

Created by Bobbie Kalman

For Caroline and Paul

Written by
Bobbie Kalman

Coordinating editor
Ellen Rodger

Editor
Jane Lewis

Contributing editors
Kate Calder
P.A. Finlay
Carrie Gleason

Editors/first edition
Greg Nickles
Niki Walker
Dave Schimpky

Production coordinator
Rose Gowsell

Design and production
Text Etc.

Separations and film
Quadratone Graphics Ltd.

Printer
Worzalla Publishing Company

Consultant
Nancy Tingley, Wattis Curator
of Southeast Asian Art, Asian Art
Museum of San Francisco

Special thanks to
Marc Crabtree, who, during a recent assignment in
Vietnam, took photographs that gave an accurate
portrayal of modern Vietnam; Lance Woodruff

Photographs
Alison Wright/Photo Researchers: p. 1; Samantha
Brown: p. 3, 10, 14, 16, 20 (bottom), 21 (top), 23 (top),
29 (top); Marc Crabtree: p. 5, 6 (top & middle), 11
(both), 12, 13 (top), 15 (both), 17 (bottom), 18 (both),
19, 20 (top), 21 (bottom), 24, 26, 27, 29 (bottom);
Jean-Leo Dugast/Panos Pictures: p. 4; John R.
Jones/Corbis/Magmaphoto: p. 8 (both); Wolfgang
Kaehler: p. 17 (top), 28; Catherine Karnow/ Corbis/
Magmaphoto: p. 9 (bottom); Noboru Komine/Photo
Researchers: p. 13 (bottom); Michael McDonell: p. 7, 9
(top); Tim Page/ Corbis/Magmaphoto: p. 23
(bottom); Caroline Penn/Panos Pictures: p. 6
(bottom); Steve Raymer/ Corbis/Magmaphoto: p. 22;
Paul Stepan-Vierow/Photo Researchers: p. 25;
Nevada Wier/Corbis/Magmaphoto: cover

Every effort has been made to obtain the appropriate credit
and full copyright clearance for all images in this book. Any
oversights, despite Crabtree's greatest precautions, will be
corrected in future editions.

Illustrations
Renné Benoit: p. 30–31
Scott Mooney: icons
David Wysotski, Allure Illustrations: back cover

Cover: Theater is an important part of Vietnamese
culture. A performer fixes her costume before the show.

Title page: A Buddhist temple in the city of Dalat,
in central Vietnam. The majority of Vietnamese
people are Buddhists.

Icon: A statue of the Buddha, founder of the
Buddhist religion.

Back cover: Water buffalo are used in farming.

Published by
Crabtree Publishing Company

PMB 16A,   612 Welland Avenue   73 Lime Walk
350 Fifth Avenue   St. Catharines   Headington
Suite 3308   Ontario, Canada   Oxford OX3 7AD
New York   L2M 5V6   United Kingdom
N.Y. 10118

Cataloging in Publication Data
Kalman, Bobbie, 1947-
    Vietnam. The culture / Bobbie Kalman.-- Rev. ed.
      p. cm. -- (The Lands, peoples, and cultures series)
    Includes index.
    Summary: Describes such aspects of Vietnamese culture
as theater, music and dance, architecture, religion, festivals, and
foods.
    ISBN 0-7787-9357-5 (RLB) -- ISBN 0-7787-9725-2 (pbk.)
    1. Vietnam--Civilization--Juvenile literature. [1.
Vietnam--Civilization.] I. Title. II. Series.
DS556.42 .K34 2002
959.7--dc21
                                           2001047108
                                           LC

Contents

 # Yesterday and today

Vietnam's culture reaches back to the Viet people who lived in the Red River Delta area of northern Vietnam over 2000 years ago. Although many of today's customs and traditions are uniquely Vietnamese, several features of the culture came from other places. Throughout Vietnam's long history, foreign peoples introduced their way of life and customs into Vietnamese culture.

The Chinese ruled Vietnam for hundreds of years and had a great influence on its culture. The Vietnamese adopted Chinese religions, writing symbols, and medical practices. Through trade, India and the once-powerful **Cham** and **Khmer** peoples also influenced Vietnamese society. French **colonial** rulers brought their European beliefs and customs in the nineteenth century. During the war between North and South Vietnam, Americans also introduced their way of life to the Vietnamese.

A culture controlled

In 1975, the entire country of Vietnam was united under a communist government. Communism is the theory that all property and businesses should be controlled by the government, and that wealth and goods should be distributed equally among the people. For just over a decade, most of Vietnam's businesses

were owned by the government. Art, television, literature, and theater were also government controlled. Communist leaders tried to re-educate people to abandon their religious and **traditional** beliefs, which were seen as a threat to the community. A policy called *doi moi*, which means "new thinking," was introduced in 1986. This policy removed many economic and cultural restrictions. Today, the Vietnamese people feel more free to practice their traditional customs.

Opening to the world

For a number of years, the Vietnamese were not allowed to trade with most of the outside world. Today, the country is open to foreigners who have introduced the Vietnamese people to fashions, rock music, and food from other parts of Asia and the West. Although this new way of life has become part of everyday culture, Vietnamese families still cherish their old traditions.

(above) A group of Vietnamese rice farmers wear traditional non-la hats. Farming has been a major occupation for many generations.

(opposite page) A guard stands in front of Ho Chi Minh's mausoleum in Hanoi. Ho Chi Minh fought for Vietnamese independence from the French, and founded the Vietnamese Communist Party.

Music, theater, and dance

Vietnamese performing arts are a combination of song, drama, and dance. The music and dancing tells a story and often includes gestures. Stage performers wear brightly colored costumes and detailed makeup.

Music medley

The Vietnamese have adapted several musical styles to suit their taste. The Chinese musical tradition which is based on five tones, or notes, has had the greatest influence on Vietnamese musicians. More recently, classical music from Europe and rock music from China and North America have become popular. In cities today, it is not unusual to hear different kinds of music coming from dance clubs and open-air concerts. Music is also a major part of Vietnamese theater and dance.

Modern sounds

It is difficult for modern musicians to make a living in Vietnam. Most current pop music is produced by Vietnamese artists who have moved to the United States. Khanh Ly is one popular star who moved to California in 1975. She was the first Vietnamese singer to perform in a foreign country. Quang Linh is a popular singer who remains in Vietnam. He is known for his love songs.

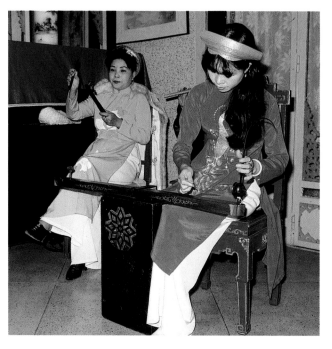

(top) The girl dressed in red is playing a dan bau zither.

(bottom left) Traditional Vietnamese instruments include zithers and long-handled guitars.

(below) Percussion and string instruments hang from the rafters at this market stall.

Instruments

Vietnamese instruments create a wide range of sounds. The **zither**, a stringed instrument, is plucked and bowed to make either sharp or wailing tones. The *dan bau*, a popular single-stringed zither, can even sound like a human voice. Flutes made of bamboo create airy, fluid notes. **Percussion** instruments, such as xylophones, drums, and bells, produce pounding and clanging beats. Drums are especially important in classical theater, where they are beaten to create different moods.

Sing out loud

Most Vietnamese music is sung, and singers are often accompanied by traditional instruments. Many Vietnamese songs are based on poetry and traditional folktales. These songs, called *hat a dao*, are about love and sadness. There are also boating songs, fishing songs, and songs workers sing to help them through long days of hard labor. Songs are also a part of play and celebration. *Trong quan* or *quan ho* songs are sung by children at some village festivals. First, boys gather and sing a challenge to girls. The girls then sing a reply to the boys. The singers invent several more verses before their song is finished.

Ceremonial music

Music is a powerful part of Vietnamese ceremonies. Weddings, funerals, and special holidays are celebrated with singers and musicians. Music is important in religious life and is often heard in **temples**. Some worshippers recite words in a low voice, as if they are chanting. Others sing their prayers in different tones. Sometimes chants are accompanied by instruments such as drums, bells, fiddles, gongs, and cymbals.

(below) Groups of people who live in the hills perform their own traditional music and dances. Here, the Black Tai tribe of the northern highlands performs a traditional dance called Xoe. In some tribes only the women dance, while in others, only the men are permitted to dance.

The theater

Theater in Vietnam often includes dancing, singing, and acting. Vietnamese dramas are colorful events that feature bright makeup and fancy costumes. Different forms of theater are *hat tuong*, *hat cheo*, *kich noi*, and *cai luong*.

The opera

Hat tuong is a traditional form of theater that was adapted from Chinese opera by the Vietnamese. In an opera, the actors sing their lines rather than speak them. The stories of *hat tuong* are based on myths and legends. Audiences can recognize characters by their costumes, makeup, and gestures, which are the same in each performance. Makeup is used to show the traits of a character. For example, gold makeup signifies a god, whereas black makeup means that a character is brave.

(above) Hat tuong *is classical Vietnamese opera.*

(below) An opera performer applies her makeup before the show.

Playing for laughs

Hat cheo theater is a comical version of *hat tuong*. It tells traditional stories in a lighthearted way. It features funny scenes, folk songs, and dance, and sometimes pokes fun at Vietnamese society. A character called *he cheo*, which means "the buffoon," appears in most *hat cheo* performances.

Modern forms

Cai luong theater has been extremely popular since it was invented in the early 1900s. Many troupes, or groups of actors, specialize in this kind of comedy. *Cai luong* shows are similar to North American musicals. Surprisingly, all of the songs in *cai luong* theater have developed from one traditional love song called *Vong Co*. Its melody can be heard throughout any performance. *Kich noi* is another modern form of theater in Vietnam. It is a type of spoken drama that was invented in the 1920s. *Kich noi* was not originally popular in Vietnam because it does not have dancing or singing.

(above) **These actors belong to a cai luong theater troupe. Children sometimes perform in these musical plays.**

(above) **These cai luong *actors are dressed to portray heroes and gods in a musical performance.***

Puppet shows

The theater art of puppetry has been popular in Vietnam for centuries. Shadow puppet shows use shadows to act out ancient stories of adventure. Water puppetry, called *roi nuoc*, is unique because its "stage" is a small pond. From behind a backdrop, puppeteers move strings, wires, and bamboo poles to make the wooden puppets glide on the water. The audience, sitting on the shore, watches the puppets appear and disappear into water.

Water puppets

Puppet makers and puppeteers are skilled and respected artists who spend years perfecting their talents. The wooden puppets only last about three to four months because they become damaged from being in water all the time. The puppet makers create characters such as princes, princesses, peasants, demons, and monkeys.

Ancient stories

Water puppetry is believed to have been invented centuries ago when an ordinary puppet show was suddenly interrupted by one of Vietnam's many floods! The puppeteers started performing shows in the water all the time. The stories are accompanied by musicians who play flutes and drums to set the mood for each scene. The puppets act out stories of ancient myths and legends. Some of the puppets are very amusing and make the audience howl with laughter.

(above) Some water puppets are set on a floating base, such as this dragon boat. A pole attached to the base lets a puppeteer move the puppets from behind the backdrop.

Shadow puppets

To perform a shadow puppet show, flat puppets are cut from pieces of leather in the shapes of people and animals. When evening comes, a light is shone behind a large screen of white cloth. The audience sits on the other side of the screen. Music begins to play. While a narrator tells the story, the puppeteers create shadows by holding up their puppets behind the screen. The shadows dance and seem to come alive. In a traditional shadow puppet show, an entire story stretches over seven nights!

(above) Water puppeteers stand waist-deep in water, hidden behind a backdrop called a puppet house.

(right) Water puppets are carved from wood and painted by skillful artisans. The puppets can weigh as much as 33 pounds (15 kilograms) each.

11

Traces of Chinese, Indian, French, and American influences on Vietnam's culture can be seen in the country's remarkable variety of building styles, or architecture. Unfortunately, many structures were destroyed during the wars and battles that have taken place in Vietnam. The Vietnamese people have worked to rebuild and repair these buildings that are such an important part of their country's past.

Cham structures

From 100 to 1600 A.D., the coast of central Vietnam belonged to a separate kingdom called Champa. The Cham people built cities with palaces, temples, and homes. Over the centuries, most of these buildings were reduced to ruins, but some of the temples still stand. These red brick structures look like tall, narrow towers. Most have three stories, or levels, each one smaller than the one beneath. Detailed sculptures decorate the inside and outside of these temples.

Pagodas

Some of the most elaborate buildings in Vietnam are the Chinese-style temples called **pagodas**. Most of the pagodas are hundreds of years old and have been restored over the years. They are decorated with sculptures and brightly painted wood. The inside of a pagoda is decorated with beautiful statues and inscriptions. Statues of Buddha, the founder of Buddhism, and bodhisattvas, or Buddhist holy people, are found in and around pagodas. Most pagodas also have a statue of the Jade Emperor, the ruler of all gods in the Taoist religion.

The Hué Citadel

In the early 1800s, Emperor Gia Long of the Nguyen dynasty ordered the construction of a citadel, or walled fortress, in the city of Hué. It took thousands of **artisans** and laborers many years to complete this enormous project. The Citadel's design was based on the Forbidden City in Beijing, China. Architects designed the Citadel to be a strong fortress as well as a magnificent residence for Vietnamese emperors.

Three cities in one

Inside the Citadel's thick outer wall, a second wall, the Imperial Enclosure, was built. Inside the Imperial Enclosure was the Forbidden Purple City, which was the emperor's residence. These two walls divided Hué into three small "cities." Artisans and merchants lived in the first city, which was just inside the outer wall. The middle city had temples and libraries and was home to court officials and Buddhist monks. The Forbidden Purple City was only for the emperor, his family, and his closest advisors.

(left) A beautifully decorated Cham tower stands in ruins. Champa's culture was strongly influenced by traders from India, and Cham architecture resembles the Hindu architecture found in India.

French architecture

When the French ruled Vietnam in the nineteenth century, they built many buildings in cities such as Hanoi, Da Nang, and Ho Chi Minh City. These cities were the centers of French government, and the impressive buildings were a display of French power. Today, these beautiful French-style buildings still line the wide **boulevards** of large cities. Shuttered windows, intricate ironwork, and pastel yellow colors are among the features of French colonial architecture. The French also built churches and cathedrals so that European and Vietnamese Catholics would have places for worship.

Modern developments

Many buildings were damaged or destroyed during the Vietnam War in the 1960s and 1970s. The ruins were left to crumble for many years. Recently, the government has restored many of these damaged buildings to increase tourism. New buildings in Vietnam are built to be modern and practical. Skyscrapers and large apartment buildings are built in and around cities. Smaller residential homes are often made of concrete and aluminum.

(above) The French influenced the architecture of many buildings in Hanoi and Ho Chi Minh City.

(below) The Thai Hoa Palace, or the Palace of Supreme Peace, was part of the Forbidden Purple City of Hué. It was used by the emperor for important receptions and ceremonies.

Arts and crafts

For thousands of years, Vietnamese artisans have created beautiful handicrafts. Their ancient skills have been handed down from generation to generation. Children first learn these skills by watching their parents work. When they have enough knowledge of the craft, the children begin perfecting their skills by working as **apprentices** to their parents.

Some villages are known for the special art created by the people who live there. In Hanoi, there is an area called 36 streets that has a community of artists. Each street features artisans who specialize in one craft.

Ceramics

During the rule of the Chinese, from 111 B.C. to 939 A.D., Vietnamese artisans learned how to create glazed pottery, or ceramics. The art of making ceramics is still popular today. A family often has its own workshop where potters mold clay into vases, dishes, and cups. The clay items are baked in a large oven called a kiln until they harden and turn white. The pottery is then painted with a glaze and baked again. The kiln's intense heat melts the glaze and, as it cools, it forms a layer of colored glass over the pottery. The most famous Vietnamese ceramics are those decorated with delicate blue and white designs.

(above) This skilled weaver creates beautiful cloth using a loom.

Working in wood

For centuries, craftspeople have carved the hardwoods of the rainforest into ornate boxes and statues. Creating lacquerware is another traditional woodworking art. Lacquerware items, such as vases and furniture, are made of wood and decorated with paint or with inlaid designs of gold, silver, mother-of-pearl, or eggshell. Their surfaces are covered with lacquer, which comes from the sap of the *son* tree. Lacquer adds to the rich colors and grains of hardwoods and makes them shine. Artisans apply ten coats of lacquer to the wooden crafts. Each coat takes seven days to dry!

Weaving

Many rural and mountain peoples practice the art of weaving. They create colorful blankets and clothing on traditional looms. People in the country also weave straw, grass, and rice stalks into hats, baskets, and mats. They even weave round boats out of bamboo.

Silk

The city of Hoi An was once a center of silk production. To make silk, the strands of a silkworm's cocoon are unraveled. The strands are then weaved together to produce the material. Traditionally, Vietnamese officials wore silk robes to show their importance. European traders who visited Hoi An eagerly bought Vietnamese silk. Silk was also used as canvas for paintings. Traditional silk paintings date back to the 1200s. Nguyen Phan Chanh is a modern artist who helped revive this delicate art form. Silk painting has regained popularity in Vietnam.

Modern art

Vietnam's art culture grew quickly after *doi moi* was introduced in 1986. New art galleries opened in cities across the country, displaying the works of talented Vietnamese artists. Trinh Tuan is an artist from Hanoi who uses the traditional style of lacquer painting to create modern images. In recent years, Trinh Tuan and many other modern Vietnamese artists have gained international recognition for their work.

(above) Modern artists in Vietnam are creating their own unique styles using elements of traditional Vietnamese and European art.

(below) This fantastic dragon boat and the laughing Buddha statue were carved from wood.

Religion and beliefs

The religious beliefs of the ancient Vietnamese are known as animism. Animism is the belief that all living and non-living things have a spirit. Taoist and Confucian beliefs were brought to Vietnam by Chinese rulers. Around 100 A.D., monks from neighboring countries introduced Buddhism to the Vietnamese. Most people in Vietnam follow a mix of animistic, Confucian, Taoist, and Buddhist beliefs. Belief in a combination of these religions is called Tam Giao, or Triple Religion.

Mahayana Buddhism

Most Vietnamese are Buddhists. Buddhism was introduced to the people of Vietnam from India and China. Buddhists believe that each person lives many lives. The cycle of living and dying ends only when a person reaches nirvana, or ultimate peace. Buddhists believe that a great teacher named Gautama Buddha reached nirvana through meditation.

Most Vietnamese practice a form of Buddhism called Mahayana Buddhism. Its followers vow to protect all life, and work toward reaching nirvana. Living **saints** who have reached nirvana are called bodhisattvas. They show patience and compassion toward others and help them reach nirvana. Buddhists offer prayers to these holy people.

Taoism

Taoism, pronounced "dowism," also came to Vietnam from China. Taoism is based on the philosophy of a man named Lao Tse, who wrote a short book called *Tao Te Ching*. Lao Tse taught that the way to find peace is to live a simple life in harmony with nature. In Vietnam, the Taoist religion centers around the Jade Emperor, who is the ruler over all the gods.

Taoists believe that there is a **universal** force present in all things. The symbol of this force is the yin yang circle, which is called *am duong* in Vietnamese. The black and white halves of the circle symbolize that opposite things, such as good and evil, hot and cold, and sweet and sour, exist together. When these opposites are in balance, the body and soul are at peace.

(left) The entrance to Ngoc Son Temple in Hanoi.

(opposite page, bottom) Taoists offer burning incense in memory of the dead.

Confucianism

Confucius was a Chinese teacher who was born around 550 B.C. He believed that education was very important. He taught people to honor their parents, government leaders, and teachers. For hundreds of years, the Vietnamese government was based on the teachings of Confucius. His ideas still play a strong role in everyday life. Vietnamese beliefs about the importance of education, family structure, and social responsibilities are rooted in Confucianism.

Ancestor worship

The worship of **ancestors** is an important part of Confucian and Taoist beliefs. People believe that the soul lives on after death and remains on earth to protect its descendants. The Vietnamese honor their dead relatives regularly, especially on the anniversary of their death. Most homes have **altars** where people can pray and make offerings to their ancestors. They believe that, in return, the spirits of their ancestors will help them achieve success in school or business.

(above) Worshippers who come to the Vinh Trang Pagoda in southern Vietnam pray in front of these statues of Buddha.

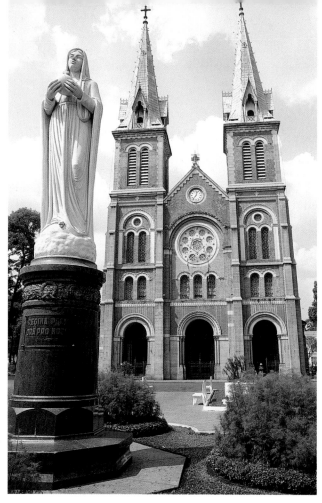

Christianity

When Europeans began traveling to Vietnam in the 1500s, missionaries came to spread Roman Catholicism, which is a Christian faith. Christians follow the teachings of Jesus Christ, who they believe was the son of God on earth. Many Vietnamese chose to become Catholic even though they were punished by the emperors, who were against the teachings of the missionaries. Roman Catholicism spread during French rule, and today ten percent of the Vietnamese population is Christian.

(left) The Notre Dame Cathedral in Ho Chi Minh City serves those who follow the Catholic faith.

(below) The center of the Cao Dai faith is a large, colorful temple in the town of Long Hoa, near Ho Chi Minh City. Here, worshippers sit inside the Cao Dai Great Temple to pray. Prayer ceremonies occur four times a day.

Cao Dai

The Cao Dai faith originated in Vietnam in the early 1920s. It was founded by a **mystic** named Ngo Minh Chieu. Today, more than two million people follow this religion. They believe in one God, who has a female **counterpart** called the Mother Goddess. The followers of Cao Dai accept the lessons of **Muhammad**, Jesus, Buddha, and many other religious teachers.

Good and bad luck

Some Vietnamese believe that much of their good or bad fortune is a matter of luck. They consult the stars and constantly watch for signs that will give them clues about their future. They also hire experts to tell them exactly how to build and furnish their houses to assure prosperity and good luck. This practice is known as geomancy. Vietnamese believe that there are countless ways to influence luck. For example, the number nine is very lucky. Seeing a bat or passing a funeral also means good luck is on its way. Seeing chopsticks stand upright in a bowl of rice, though, could mean death is in the near future. The chopsticks remind people of **incense** sticks, which are burned for ancestors in the temples.

Watching the stars

Astrology is the belief that the stars affect people's lives and can show the future. In Vietnam and other Asian countries, a person's date of birth is important because, according to astrology, it decides his or her character and destiny. Experts in astrology, called astrologers, are consulted to foretell a person's future based on his or her date of birth. Some people make important decisions based on these predictions.

Religion and government

Officially, Vietnamese people have freedom of religion. However, the government does not allow religious practices that may interfere with the country's laws or hamper a person's work. For example, the government limits the production of Christian literature because some Christian teachings contradict communist beliefs. The government also forbids superstitious practices, such as astrology and geomancy. These practices, however, are a deep part of the Vietnamese culture.

(above) Two Cao Dai worshippers at the temple.

A life of devotion

Most Vietnamese cities, towns, and villages have a pagoda which is the center of the community's spiritual life. Many Vietnamese follow Buddhist beliefs and contribute a portion of their earnings to support the monks and nuns who look after pagodas.

Monks and nuns are Buddhist men and women who devote their entire lives to their religion. In Vietnam, monks are called *bhiksu* and nuns are called *bhiksuni*. In some countries, Buddhist monks and nuns live in their own religious communities. In Vietnam, they have important and active roles in community life.

(right) These nuns, who devote their lives to Buddhism, are preparing a meal. There are more than 11,000 Buddhist nuns in Vietnam.

Wearing robes

Monks and nuns wear robes and keep their hair very short. Monks usually wear gray or brown robes, but they dress in yellow robes for special occasions. Nuns wear white robes. Monks and nuns cannot own anything, so they must rely on the people who visit the pagoda to give them food and other necessary supplies.

Becoming a monk

There are several different stages of becoming a monk. Beginner monks are called novices. After a monk turns twenty, he can write a difficult exam on Buddhist beliefs. If he passes, he is raised to the second level. Years of further study are required before the monk is ready to write an exam to reach the third level. Monks who pass this exam are honored with the title "Thich." Even more highly honored are the few monks who reach the fourth and fifth levels.

A monk's life

A monk's day begins early in the morning with prayers and the study of Buddhist teachings. The first meal of the day is eaten at noon. Buddhist monks do not eat meat because harming animals is forbidden. They eat rice, vegetables, and **tofu**. After this meal, the monks rest for a while. In the afternoon, there is more study time. Some monks work in the community, visiting sick people or performing ceremonies in the pagoda. After dinner, there is evening prayer. Before going to bed, the monks have time to relax or go for walks. They spend the night sleeping on simple mats.

(above) The monk at this temple gives a friendly greeting to visitors.

(right) The founder of the Buddhist faith, the Buddha, is represented by the golden statue on this altar.

(opposite page, bottom) An old pagoda in Ho Chi Minh City provides a quiet place where worshippers can get away from the noise of the city.

Family celebrations

Families celebrate important events together, such as birthdays and weddings. The family is very important in Vietnamese culture. Being part of a family provides happiness and support. The Vietnamese honor the events in the life of every family member. Even after death, a family member is honored and continues to play an important role in a loved one's life.

Baby's first birthday

A baby's first birthday is the most exciting event for new parents. Family and friends are invited to a party where the parents officially introduce the baby with his or her given name. After this first party, a person's individual birthday is no longer celebrated. Instead, people honor their birthday on Tet, the Vietnamese new year, when everyone becomes one year older.

Wedding bells

A wedding is an exciting and joyous event. In the past, an older, respected husband and wife often acted as **matchmakers** for a young couple. Matchmakers helped choose husbands or wives and also helped arrange a wedding. They consulted an astrologer to decide on the best dates for the engagement party and wedding ceremony. Today, couples are free to choose their partners, but many still consult astrologers. If the stars are in a lucky position on the day of the wedding ceremony, the couple is expected to have a happy marriage.

(above) A bride and groom enter a temple in Ho Chi Minh City as part of their wedding ceremony. They are wearing the traditional red and blue ao dais of a Vietnamese wedding.

The engagement party

At the engagement party, the bride's and groom's families are officially introduced. The groom makes a formal request for permission to marry the bride. He presents the woman's family with betel leaves and areca nuts. The young couple receives many gifts at the engagement party. Some are supposed to bring the couple good luck, whereas others are objects that the couple will need to begin their life together. The groom presents his future wife with a tray of gold engagement jewelry.

Tying the knot

On the day of the ceremony, a traditional bride wears a special pink or red *ao dai*, and the groom wears a blue one. The couple stands in front of a family altar, and an elder lights two red candles. The couple then eats a piece of ginger dipped in salt. Its unpleasant taste represents the challenges the couple will face together. The bride and groom exchange rings, and their hands are tied together with a pink thread, which symbolizes their happiness. Everyone then gathers at the groom's home for the wedding feast.

Changing traditions

Today, many weddings are based on **Western**, rather than Vietnamese, traditions. Instead of an *ao dai*, the bride wears a white wedding gown, and the groom wears a suit. Some couples exchange their vows in a church rather than in front of their family altar.

Celebrating loved ones

Although the death of a relative is a sad event for Vietnamese families, it is also a time to remember and celebrate that person's life. Loved ones are remembered long after the funeral. Their pictures are placed on the family altar, and each year a feast is held to honor the relative's departure to the spirit world.

(top) This young couple has chosen a modern, Western-style wedding.

(right) A grand procession is part of a traditional Vietnamese funeral.

Festivals

The Vietnamese people have many festivals throughout the year, celebrating religious feasts, ancestors, and the changing of the seasons. Firecrackers, colorful lanterns, fresh flowers, delicious foods, and sweet-smelling incense are often part of the festivities.

Watch the moon

Today, most people use a **solar** calendar which has 365 days in each year. This calendar measures the length of time it takes the earth to orbit the sun once. In the past, the Vietnamese followed a **lunar** calendar. The calendar was based on the cycles of the moon and had 155 days in each year. This lunar calendar is still used to calculate the dates of traditional Vietnamese holidays.

Time for Tet!

Tet Nguyen Dan, or Tet, is the most important festival of the year in Vietnam. It is the traditional lunar new year and marks the beginning of spring. Tet is also the day when all Vietnamese celebrate their birthday and become one year older. People take part in colorful parades, feasts, dances, and family gatherings. Tet falls near the end of January or early February and the festivities often last for more than a week. The festival is officially celebrated for only three days. Workers and students are given these days off so they can enjoy the holiday.

Getting ready

Preparations begin weeks before Tet. People make plans to travel home for the holiday, even from overseas. To start the year off right, people buy new clothes, repay debts, and settle arguments. Everyone pitches in to make sure the house is spotless before the guests arrive. It is especially important that the family shrine is clean because the spirits of ancestors are honored during the festival.

(left) Happy New Year balloons can be seen everywhere during Tet. This young boy is waiting eagerly for the coming parade.

A flowery festival

A popular Tet custom is to decorate the house with flowers. Apricot and plum blossoms, chrysanthemums, and other fresh flowers are placed throughout homes as a symbol of the new spring. Budding branches of the *hao moi* tree are cut and brought indoors. If they bloom before Tet begins, the family can expect to have good luck for the year.

Housekeeping reports

Another Tet tradition is to get ready for the visit of Ong Tao, the kitchen spirit. Legend says that on New Year's day, Ong Tao flies from earth to the Jade Emperor, the ruler of all gods. He brings the Jade Emperor reports on each family's housekeeping. A good report brings good luck for the year, so families leave Ong Tao gifts of fruit, honey, and paper money in their kitchens. A paper fish is also left for Ong Tao so he can ride it back to the home of the gods.

The night before Tet

On the eve of Tet, families gather for a large meal. A favorite treat is *banh chung*, a small rice cake, wrapped in banana leaves, with sweet bean paste and pork in the center. Other special Tet foods include fried watermelon seeds, dried fruit, candy, and pickled vegetables. Families include their ancestors in this feast by placing food on the family altar. A stick of incense is lit on the altar. When the incense is finished burning, it is seen as a sign that the ancestors have "finished eating." The rest of the family then begins their meal.

(above) A dragon puppet is part of the New Year festivities in the Kien Giang province in southern Vietnam. There, the Tet festival is celebrated with a parade called the Unicorn Dance.

Ringing in the new year

At midnight, the lunar new year begins with a bang! People make as much noise as they can with drums and rattles to welcome the new year and scare away evil spirits. When the new year comes, the problems from the previous year are left behind.

Starting off right

The first day of the new year is very important because whatever happens on this day will affect the rest of the year. It is also a time for visiting. To ensure good luck, each family invites a respected person to be the first visitor of the year. Special greetings, written in the ancient *chu nom* script, are sent to friends and neighbors. If children were well-behaved in the previous year, they receive gifts of money wrapped in red rice paper.

Holidays for the dead

The Doan Ngu festival marks the longest day of the year—the summer **solstice**. It occurs during the fifth lunar month. On this solemn day, paper **effigies** are burned as offerings to the god of death to appease him and prevent the spread of diseases.

The festival of Trung Nguyen begins in the seventh lunar month and lasts for a month. It is believed that during this time the souls of the dead wander the earth. People make offerings of food and incense to their ancestors to give them comfort during their travels.

Harvest moon

During the eighth lunar month, the mid-autumn festival, or Tet Trung-thu, is held to celebrate the harvest. This festival is also called the Moon Festival because the full moon is largest and brightest at this time of year. Children celebrate Tet Trung-thu by making ricepaper lanterns, which are hung on long bamboo poles. Some lanterns are shaped like stars or fish, and others are covered in fancy designs. After dark, the candles inside the lanterns are lit, and the children march in a colorful parade. They carefully protect their lanterns from the wind. To reach the end of the parade without the lantern catching fire is a real challenge! After the parade, children return home to a treat of moon cakes, made with rice, peanuts, raisins, watermelon seeds, and eggs.

Honoring heroes

Many festivals celebrate heroes in Vietnam's history. For example, Ho Chi Minh's birthday is a public holiday held on May 19. The Trung Sisters Festival is another national celebration. It is held to honor the two women who overthrew the Chinese rulers in 39 A.D. Each town and village chooses two girls to dress up in colorful costumes like those worn by the sisters. The girls ride through the streets, reminding people of the important contributions women have made to Vietnam's history.

(left) Flowers symbolize the new year, new growth, and the coming of spring.

(opposite page) In some Vietnamese festivals, people dress in historical costumes.

Flavors of Vietnam

Food is an important part of every culture. For the Vietnamese, who have experienced many periods of **famine**, having enough food to eat is especially important. Rice and vegetables are part of every meal. Fish, meat, or tofu are sometimes added. Chinese and French cooking methods have influenced the cuisine, but there are many flavors that are strictly Vietnamese, such as fish sauce.

Regional variations

Different areas of Vietnam have their own tastes. Northern Vietnam has many stir-fried dishes similar to Chinese cuisine. Cooks in central Vietnam use a lot of chili in their meals. In the southern regions, many Indian spices are used, adding a distinct flavor. Seafood, an important part of the Vietnamese diet, is served throughout the country. Some restaurants feature exotic dishes, such as cobra, bat, and lizard meat!

Rice, rice, rice

Rice is Vietnam's most important crop and popular food. Plain, white, steamed rice is a part of almost every meal. Rice noodles are made of rice kernels that are ground up into flour and made into thin noodles. Rice flour is also made into rice paper, a thin sheet in which meat and vegetables are wrapped into a spring roll.

Eating Vietnamese-style

Meals are cooked on a clay or brick stove heated with charcoal or wood. The family gathers around a low table or, in the country, around a straw mat on the floor. Rice is served in individual bowls, and bite-sized pieces of meat and vegetables are served in communal dishes. Pork is a more popular meat than chicken or beef, and duck is saved for special occasions. Shrimp is a favorite seafood. People use chopsticks to eat most dishes.

Fish sauce

Fish sauce is added to almost every Vietnamese dish. It is made from salted fish, which are fermented in a vat for months. *Nuoc cham* is a tasty, mild form of the sauce made with equal parts of fish sauce and water. Many foods are dipped in *nuoc cham*. Vinegar, garlic, sugar, and chili are often added for extra flavor.

Finger food

When you eat Vietnamese spring rolls, it is not impolite to use your fingers—it is necessary! Spring rolls are made of seafood, meat, vegetables, and egg, wrapped in rice paper and fried. The spring roll is rolled up in a leaf of lettuce along with mint, cucumber, and shredded carrot. It is then dipped in *nuoc cham*. This tasty treat can be eaten as an appetizer or a snack.

(left) Most Vietnamese buy fresh food every day at a market. Few people have refrigerators to keep food from spoiling.

Wake up! Soup's on!

Pho is a noodle soup that is enjoyed at any time of the day, but most people eat it for breakfast. If you want to make this tasty soup, ask an adult for help.

Ingredients:
4 ounces (100 g) of vermicelli or rice noodles
3 ounces (85 g) of beef (sliced thin)
3 cups (750 ml) beef broth
2 medium onions, diced
2 tablespoons (30 ml) fish sauce
1/2 tablespoon (8 ml) vinegar
1 tablespoon (15 ml) minced ginger
1/2 teaspoon (2.5 ml) salt

Bring broth to a boil and add onion, ginger, salt, vinegar, and fish sauce. Simmer for ten minutes. Add noodles and boil until they are soft. Add the beef, then simmer for one minute. Remove the soup from heat. Garnish with basil, chili peppers, and fresh mint for extra flavor.

(above) To eat soup, the Vietnamese use chopsticks to eat the noodles and a spoon for the broth.

Sweet delights

Vietnamese desserts usually consist of beans, fruit, and sweet, sticky rice wrapped up in leaves. Coconuts and bananas, which grow in the south, are used in many desserts. One popular dessert is fried bananas. Try them with ice cream or honey.

Ingredients:
2 large, firm bananas, sliced lengthwise
into three pieces
1/4 cup (65 ml) milk
1 egg
1 tablespoon (15 ml) brown sugar
1/2 cup (125 ml) flour
icing sugar
vegetable or peanut oil for frying

Mix together milk, egg, sugar, and flour. Pour the mixture into a shallow bowl and dip the bananas into it. Ask an adult to heat a pan and pour in some oil. When the oil is hot, place the bananas in the pan, using tongs. Remove the bananas when they turn brown. Place them on a paper towel to cool. Sprinkle with icing sugar.

(below) The French introduced many foods to Vietnam. Today, stands selling baguettes, pastries, and croissants are found in many markets.

The story of Tam and Cam

This folktale may remind you of another popular Western folktale—Cinderella. Almost every culture around the world has a version of this tale, which is believed to have originally come from China. Here is the Vietnamese version.

A long time ago, there lived a kind and beautiful girl named Tam. She lived with her stepmother and her half-sister, who was called Cam. Tam's stepmother treated Cam like a princess, but was very cruel to Tam. She made Tam do all the work around the house. One day, the stepmother told Tam and Cam to go fishing in a nearby pond. The girl who got the most fish would be given a beautiful new shawl. Tam worked hard all day, and got a basketful of fish. Cam spent the day playing and picking flowers in the field. At the end of the day, Cam told Tam that she had better wash herself in the pond before going home, because she was covered in mud. While Tam was bathing, Cam stole the fish from her basket and went home to claim the prize. When Tam discovered that she had been tricked, she burst into tears. Her stepmother would be angry with her for not bringing home any fish, and she would not believe that Cam had stolen all her fish.

While she was crying, the Buddha appeared and gave Tam a magic fish. He told her to put the fish in the well beside her house and feed it a little rice every day. Tam went home and did just that. Every day, the fish would appear at the surface of the pond when Tam came to feed it. One day, the stepmother told Tam to take the water buffalo out to graze in the field. While the girl was away, the stepmother dressed in Tam's clothing and went to the pond. The fish appeared, and she caught it and cooked it for dinner. When Tam returned, she saw what had happened. As she wept over the lost fish, the Buddha appeared again. He told her to bury the bones of the magic fish under her sleeping mat, and to dig up the bones on the night of Tet Trung-thu—the harvest festival.

Later that month, the Emperor announced that there would be a large party for Tet Trung-thu. On the night of the festival, Tam's stepmother handed her a huge basket of white and black beans. She told Tam that she could go to the party after separating all the white beans from the black beans. Cam and the stepmother dressed in their fanciest clothes and left for the celebration.

Tam sat down with a heavy heart. She would never be able to sort all those beans. Just then, a flock of birds arrived and began to separate the beans. Tam watched with amazement as the job was finished in just a few minutes. Then she remembered the Buddha's message, and went to dig up the fish bones. Instead of fish bones, she found a beautiful dress and slippers made out of the finest cloth and sewn with gold thread. Tam put them on, and left for the party. On her way there, she lost one of the slippers.

A soldier found the slipper and brought it to the Emperor. It was so tiny and beautiful that the Emperor announced that he would marry the woman who owned it. Every woman at the festival tried on the shoe, to no avail. Finally, Tam tried it on and it fit! She also produced the matching shoe. Cam and the stepmother were jealous, and tried to stop the marriage. The Emperor knew Tam had a true heart, and they were married that night. Cam and the stepmother were driven from the land for their selfish and cruel behavior, and Tam and the Emperor lived happily together for the rest of their lives.

Glossary

altar A place where religious ceremonies are performed or offerings are made in worship

ancestor A person from whom one is descended

apprentice A person who works for an artisan in order to learn an art or craft

artisan A person who is skilled in a craft

boulevard A wide city street lined with trees

Cham Describing the culture and people associated with the former kingdom of Champa, which was in central Vietnam

colonial Describing a land or people ruled by another country

counterpart One that closely resembles and balances another

effigy An image of a hated person; effigies are usually burned

famine A period during which food is scarce

incense Wood or resin that produces a sweet-smelling smoke when burned

Khmer Describing the culture and people associated with a former empire based in what is now Cambodia and southern Vietnam

lunar Relating to the moon

matchmaker A person who brings couples together and arranges marriages

mausoleum A large tomb

Muhammad A prophet who founded a religion called Islam

mystic A person who is thought to be able to communicate with gods and spirits

pagoda A temple that is usually tower-shaped and found in eastern countries

percussion Relating to musical instruments that are played by striking

saint A person recognized by a religious faith for his or her goodness or service to others

solar Relating to the sun

solstice Either of two times in the year when the sun appears farthest from the equator

temple A place of worship

tofu A food made from soybeans

traditional Describing customs that are handed down from one generation to another

universal Relating to or affecting the whole world and universe

Western Relating to countries in the western part of the world, such as the United States or France

zither A musical instrument with one or many strings that are stretched over a stick, bar, or flat box

Index

1 2 3 4 5 6 7 8 9 0   Printed in the USA   0 9 8 7 6 5 4 3 2 1